CONTENTS

WHAT IS CODING?

How do you say hello? Think about all of the countries in the world. Does everyone speak the same language? No, there are lots of ways to say hi!

One language you may not know is a language a computer speaks – code. When you create a computer program, you are writing down what you want a computer to do in a language the computer can understand. Computers wouldn't be able to do anything if people didn't write code.

Think of coding as a set of specific directions. Those directions help a computer to do its job.

BIG IDEAS IN CODING?

As you learn to code, it is important to keep in mind three things. Those things are sequence, selection and repetition.

1. **Sequence:** Sequence is important when you are coding. Programs contain action steps. Computers run the steps of a program in the order they are written. Clear, step-by-step instructions will help the computer perform at its best.

2. **Selection:** On a bike ride, you can choose different paths to follow. When you create code, you can also make it select different paths to follow.

3. **Repetition:** Sometimes it's best to stick with what you know! You can code your computer to perform the same action many times. Computers are really good at repeating the same action.

HOW TO GET
INTO SCRATCH

All the projects in this book were created with a program called Scratch. You can create your own free account – after getting the OK from an adult – by following these steps:

1. Go to https://scratch.mit.edu

2. Find the **Join Scratch** button in the top right corner.

BE SAFE: Don't use your real name for the username. And make sure you can remember your password!

3. Create a username and password. Then press **next**.

4. Select your birthday and gender. Then choose the country you live in. Finally, press the **next** button.

This information will not be sent anywhere else.

5. If you are under 12 years old, you will need your parent's e-mail address.
If you are over 12 years old, you can use your own e-mail.

6. The fourth screen will let you know that your registration is complete!
You will receive a confirmation e-mail.

YOU CAN ALSO DOWNLOAD SCRATCH TO USE OFFLINE
Go to: https://scratch.mit.edu/scratch2download/

Click **SIGN IN** to log into your account.

Click **CREATE** to start a new project.

GETTING AROUND
IN SCRATCH!

Getting started is easy! Click around a little to get familiar with the Scratch dashboard and learn which buttons do what.

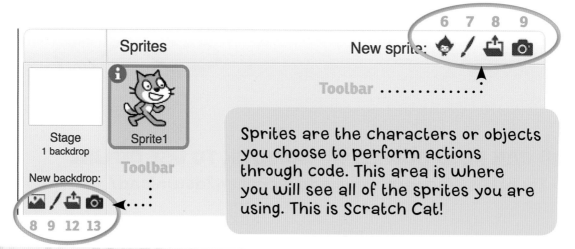

Toolbar

Scratch   File ▼ Edit ▼ Tips About   1 2 3 4

5
v457   Untitled **NAME YOUR PROJECT HERE!**
by Capstone_Publishing (unshared)

1. Make a copy of a sprite or background.
2. Delete the sprite or background.
3. Click on this tool and then onto a sprite to make the sprite larger.
4. Click on this tool and then onto a sprite to make the sprite smaller.
5. View your project full screen.
6. Pick a sprite from the library of sprites.
7. Use drawing tools and create your own sprite.

8. Upload an image to use as a sprite.
9. Take a picture and use it as a sprite.
10. Select a background from the library.
11. Use drawing tools to create your own background.
12. Upload your own background.
13. Take a picture and use it as a background.
14. View the backgrounds you are using.

Sprites   New sprite: 6 7 8 9

Stage
1 backdrop

Sprite1

Toolbar

Sprites are the characters or objects you choose to perform actions through code. This area is where you will see all of the sprites you are using. This is Scratch Cat!

New backdrop:
8 9 12 13

Toolbar

The **Scripts** tab lets you add code to any sprite or background. Click and drag the coding blocks into the large space to the right of the blocks.

The **Costumes** tab lets you view the different sprites' costumes. You can also add costumes here.

To get to the **Backdrops** tab, click the Stage button. This tab lets you see the backdrops that you are using. You can add new backdrops here as well.

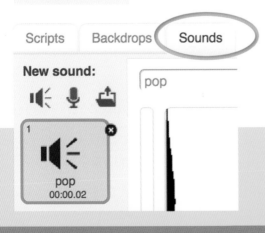

The **Sounds** tab lets you add sounds to your sprites or background. Click the little speaker to select a sound from the library. Click the microphone to record your own sound. Click the folder to upload a sound, such as a song or music file.

TIP: Even if you select a sound here, you still need to add a sound code block to hear the sound in your project.

START IT UP!

Think about how you would start a race. Would you say, "Ready, get set, go"? Or maybe you would take off after hearing a certain sound. Either way, you have to wait for a command to start running.

Just like in a race, computer programming has commands to make things start. Follow these steps to make Scratch Cat react to a start command. He will display a message, make sounds, change costumes and then disappear.

1. Start by clicking **Create** at the top left of the home page.

FOLLOW THE STEPS ON PAGE 5 TO MAKE AN ACCOUNT!

2. Select **Scratch Cat** in the Sprites section. Open his **Scripts** tab. This is where you will place code. Think of the code as directions for **Scratch Cat**.

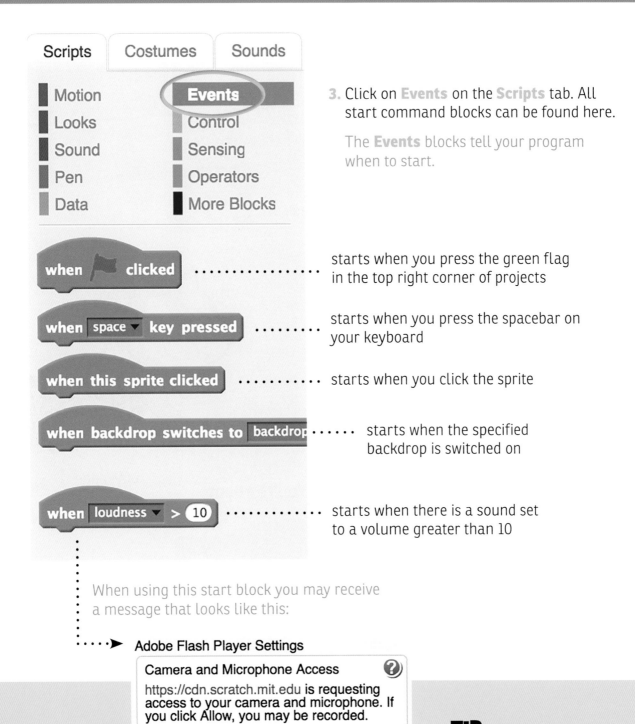

3. Click on **Events** on the **Scripts** tab. All start command blocks can be found here.

   The **Events** blocks tell your program when to start.

when ⚑ clicked .... starts when you press the green flag in the top right corner of projects

when space ▾ key pressed .... starts when you press the spacebar on your keyboard

when this sprite clicked .... starts when you click the sprite

when backdrop switches to backdrop ...... starts when the specified backdrop is switched on

when loudness ▾ > 10 .... starts when there is a sound set to a volume greater than 10

When using this start block you may receive a message that looks like this:

Adobe Flash Player Settings

Camera and Microphone Access ?

https://cdn.scratch.mit.edu is requesting access to your camera and microphone. If you click Allow, you may be recorded.

Allow   Deny

TIP: Make sure you allow access to the microphone.

Now that you know what all of the events mean, you can start using them to give your own commands. Click and drag these code blocks out into the space to create scripts.

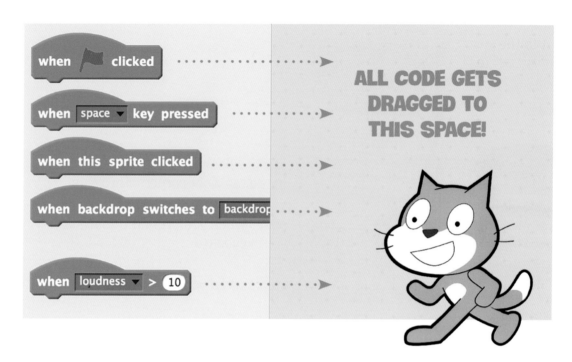

ALL CODE GETS DRAGGED TO THIS SPACE!

What noise does Scratch Cat make? You're about to find out!

Click the Sounds category. Drag out a play sound meow until done block. Attach it to the start command. When you have finished, the code will look like this:

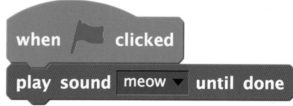

Make Scratch Cat move a little!

Click the Looks category. Add a next costume block.

When you click Scratch Cat, he will move for a moment. That's what he looks like when he switches costumes.

Make **Scratch Cat** talk! Stay in the **Looks** category and find this block ·········►

Attach it to the **loudness** start command. Change "Hello!" to "I can hear you".

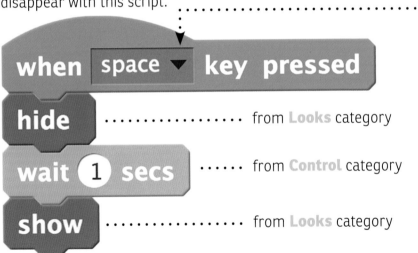

It's time for the last set of code! Make **Scratch Cat** disappear with this script.

If you press this arrow, you can pick from many different keys to start your code.

when space ▼ **key pressed**

hide ················ from **Looks** category

wait 1 secs ······ from **Control** category

show ················ from **Looks** category

EXTRAS!

See if you can change the loudness level. Does *Scratch Cat* react to a quieter sound?

Check out the *Motion* scripts. Create a program that will make *Scratch Cat* move when you click on him.

TIP: Any block in Scratch that has a white space can be edited. Just click inside the space. Then type what you want it to say.

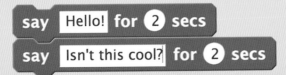

UP, DOWN, ALL AROUND!

What are key controls?

When playing digital games, the player must be able to control the characters. Key controls allow you to control your characters using code.

When you have finished this project, you will be able to code your own characters. They'll move using the keys you choose. Start by learning how to control the sprite with arrow keys. Then use your skills and make things more challenging!

1. Create a new project.
2. Click the head button to open up the library. Pick the **Butterfly1** sprite from the library.

Sprites are sorted alphabetically. You can also search by category.

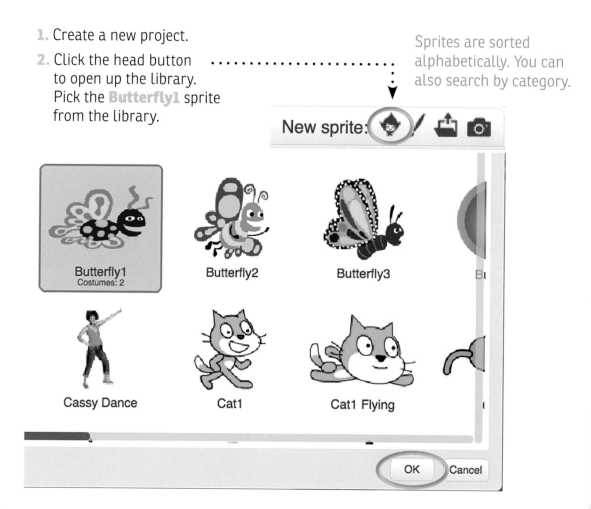

New sprite:

Butterfly1
Costumes: 2

Butterfly2

Butterfly3

Cassy Dance

Cat1

Cat1 Flying

OK   Cancel

3. Change your background. Click the button that looks like mountains. •••
Then pick **blue sky**.

New backdrop:

4. Name your project. We picked **Up, Down, All Around!**
If you don't name your project, its name will be **Untitled**.

5. Click on the **Butterfly1** sprite to select it. Make sure you are on the
Scripts tab so you can begin giving your butterfly its code.

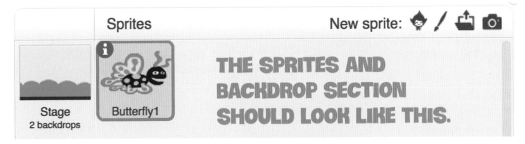

6. Change your background. Click the button that looks like mountains. Then pick **blue sky**.

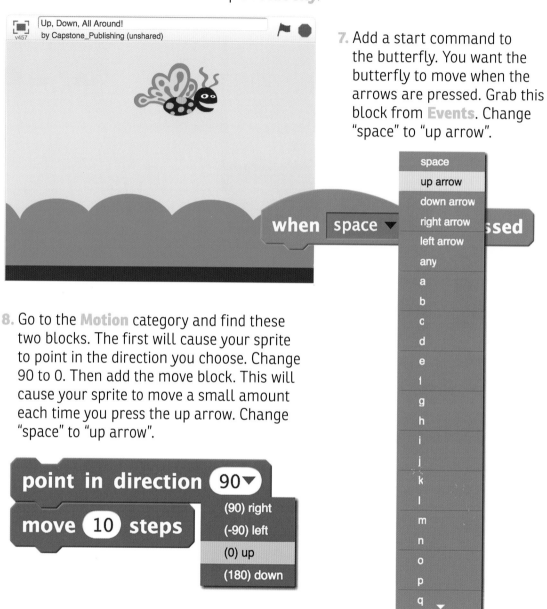

7. Add a start command to the butterfly. You want the butterfly to move when the arrows are pressed. Grab this block from **Events**. Change "space" to "up arrow".

when space ▼ ...ssed

space
up arrow
down arrow
right arrow
left arrow
any
a
b
c
d
e
f
g
h
i
j
k
l
m
n
o
p
q ▼

8. Go to the **Motion** category and find these two blocks. The first will cause your sprite to point in the direction you choose. Change 90 to 0. Then add the move block. This will cause your sprite to move a small amount each time you press the up arrow. Change "space" to "up arrow".

point in direction 90▼

move 10 steps

(90) right
(-90) left
(0) up
(180) down

9. Go to **Looks** and grab the next costume block. This block causes the sprite to switch through its costumes. As you only have two costumes, it will just move its wings up and down.

when up arrow ▼ key pressed

point in direction 90▼

move 10 steps

next costume

duplicate
delete
add comment
help

You can copy any piece of code! Right click on it and select duplicate.

10. Add code for the other arrow keys – right, left and down. Pick the correct arrow key in the start command. Make sure you change the point in direction number.

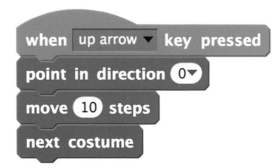

when [up arrow ▼] key pressed
point in direction (0▼)
move (10) steps
next costume

when [left arrow ▼] key pressed
point in direction (–90▼)
move (10) steps
next costume

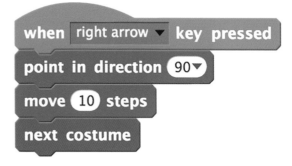

when [right arrow ▼] key pressed
point in direction (90▼)
move (10) steps
next costume

when [down arrow ▼] key pressed
point in direction (180▼)
move (10) steps
next costume

WHY IT WORKS:

The numbers next to the point in direction block may seem random. But there is a reason behind them. They are based on degrees in a circle. There are 360 degrees in total. Take a look!

$-90° = 270°$ $0° = 360°$

EXTRAS!

Change the start commands. Make the butterfly move when the A, S, D and F keys are pressed.

Change the background. Then change the sprite. A fish swimming in an ocean could be fun. Or go crazy with dancing bananas in the jungle!

SPORTS JOKES

When you text or e-mail a friend, you send them a message. Then you wait for your friend's response. The Broadcast Event script works in the same way.

In this project, you will send a message in code from one sprite to another. The second sprite will respond and react. They'll be joking back and forth in no time.

1. You will need 3 sprites. Select two Referees and one basketball from the library.

2. Select the basketball court-a background from the library.

3. Arrange your sprites on the background.

4. Click on the **Referee** sprite.

TIP: Use the shrink tool to make the basketball smaller.

continued 17

5. Select **Scripts**, and add this code:

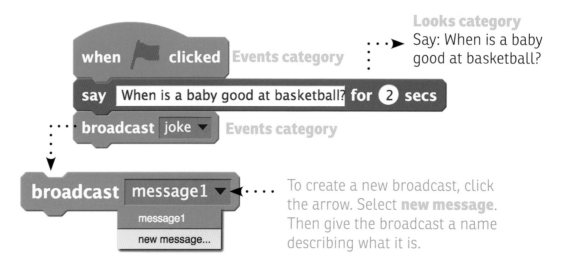

Looks category
Say: When is a baby good at basketball?

Events category

Events category

To create a new broadcast, click the arrow. Select **new message**. Then give the broadcast a name describing what it is.

6. The first sprite's broadcast will be sent to all the active sprites. Now it's up to **Referee2** to respond. Choose the **Scripts** tab. His start command will be when he receives the joke broadcast. He will receive it, respond, and then send a broadcast back. The code will look like this:

Events category When I receive: joke

Looks category
Say: Not sure, when?

Events category New broadcast: response

TIP: There's no rule for broadcast names. Just make sure they make sense to you. You should know where each broadcast is coming from. Then decide what you want to happen when they are sent.

7. **Referee** needs to reply back to **Referee2's** question. So re-select **Referee**. Then give it this script:

Events category When I receive: response

Looks category
Say: When they're DRIBBLING!

Events category New broadcast: laugh

8. **Referee** just broadcasted the rest of the joke to **Referee2**. So **Referee2** needs to laugh! Give **Referee2** this code:

Events category When I receive: laugh

Looks category
Say: Haha good one!

TIP: The messages might go too quickly for you to read. To fix this, increase the time each message is displayed for. Type a new number into the seconds bubble.

EXTRAS!

How long can you keep the joke going? Give the sprites a whole conversation!

FROG ON A
TRAMPOLINE

Think about your school routine. From Monday to Friday you get up, go to school and come home. But there's an easier way to show it. Instead of writing the same thing out five times, you can write it like this:

repeat 5 [get up, go to school, come home]

You can use repeat loops when you program too. It's an easy way to simplify or shorten a piece of code.

What is a repeat?

Monday	get up, go to school, come home
Tuesday	get up, go to school, come home
Wednesday	get up, go to school, come home
Thursday	get up, go to school, come home
Friday	get up, go to school, come home

Program a frog to jump up and down on a trampoline. Use a repeat loop for the jumps. You will use a forever loop to play music in the background.

1. Select two sprites – **Frog** and **Trampoline**.

Frog   Trampoline

2. Select the desert backdrop. Then click on the **Sounds** tab.

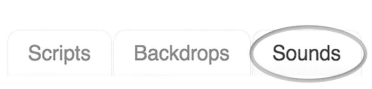

3. Click the speaker to access the library of sounds. Then select **garden**.

4. Click the **Scripts** tab. Add this code:

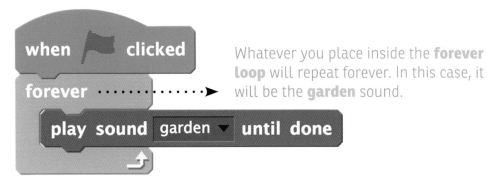

Whatever you place inside the **forever loop** will repeat forever. In this case, it will be the **garden** sound.

Press the arrow to select the correct sound. ·····················

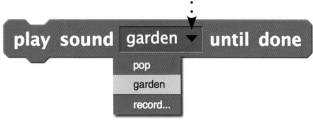

TIP: When using a sound inside a forever loop, make sure you pick the **play sound until done** block. Otherwise, the program will skip through the sound too quickly. This will make the sound choppy.

continued

5. Arrange your sprites like this on the background:

6. Add this code to the **Frog**:

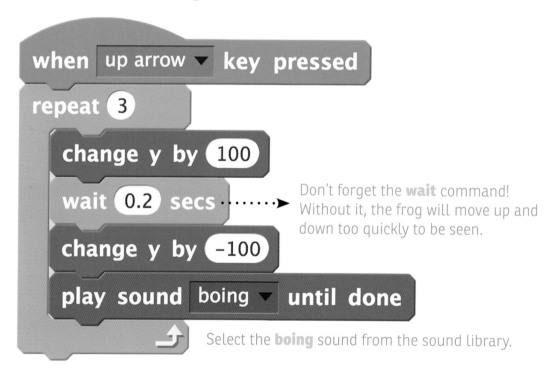

Don't forget the **wait** command!
Without it, the frog will move up and
down too quickly to be seen.

Select the **boing** sound from the sound library.

Everything inside the repeat loop will repeat. It will
follow the order that code blocks are placed.

WHY IT WORKS: Your workspace is broken up into two different axes: an x axis and a y axis. The x axis is left to right. The y axis is up and down. The y axis' number controls the frog's up and down position. If you add numbers to y, the frog will go up. If you subtract numbers from y, the frog goes down.

EXTRAS!

Play with a penguin sprite that slides from side to side.

Hint: You will need to change the x position.

MOVING
CAMPFIRE

You used a forever loop to play sound. Now use it to run a set of code non-stop.

Think about when you flip through the pages of a flipbook. Tiny changes blend together to make one moving image. You'll use a similar idea here with a sprite. The sprite will switch between costumes quickly to create the illusion of movement.

1. Click the paintbrush.

2. Use the drawing tools to make a campfire. Name your picture **Fire1**.

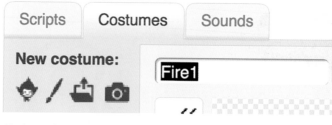

Below the tabs and above the drawing tools you will see a little white box. This is where you name your sprite.

Use the paintbrush to free draw.

 ....➤ **USE THESE**
FEATURES TO
 ....➤ **DRAW LINES,**
SQUARES OR
RECTANGLES,
 ....➤ **AND CIRCLES.**

T Use the T to create a text box to type inside.

 Use the paint bucket to fill in different areas with colour.

Use the eraser to remove parts of your drawing.

3. Use the drawing tools to create a new background that looks like a campsite.

TIP: Hold down *shift* while creating the lines, circles and squares. This will help you make a perfect line, circle or square.

4. When you have created your campfire, use the stamp button to make a copy.

New costume:

5. Change a small detail on the copy.

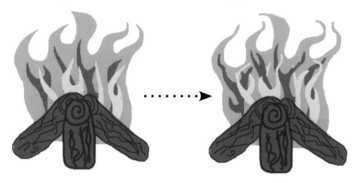

Can you see the small difference between **Fire1** and **Fire2**?

6. Once you've finished **Fire2**, stamp a copy of it to create **Fire3**. Change another small detail on the third fire.

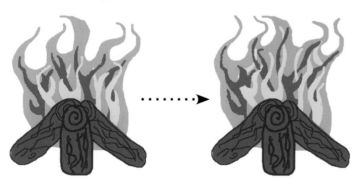

Can you see the small difference between **Fire2** and **Fire3**?

7. Make your fire move. This code will make it switch between its three costumes.

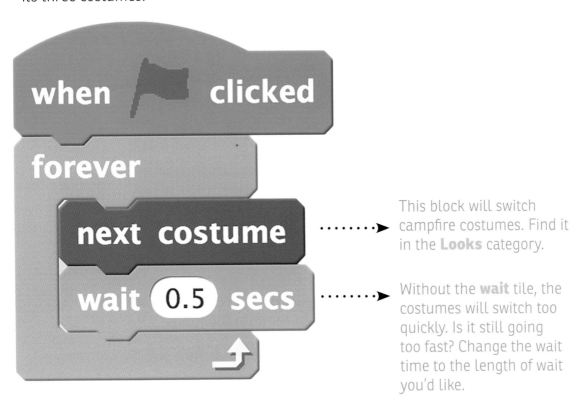

This block will switch campfire costumes. Find it in the **Looks** category.

Without the **wait** tile, the costumes will switch too quickly. Is it still going too fast? Change the wait time to the length of wait you'd like.

TIP: Use the eraser tool to remove flames. Use the paintbrush to add them.

EXTRAS!

Add additional costumes to create a more detailed campfire animation.

SPOOKY SCENE

Hopping sprites and blinking images are fun. But what if you want both? Everything happens in sequence when it is part of the same piece of code. So how can you make two things happen at the same time?

The answer is parallel processing. This is when two codes run at the same time. To do this in Scratch, you'll need to write two separate pieces of code. They will have the same start command. Think of it as the "rubbing your belly and patting your head at the same time" code!

Give parallel processing a try! Make the background change colours and play music at the same time. For extra spookiness, add a bat that will flap around the screen in random locations.

1. Select the **Bat2** sprite and **woods** backdrop.

2. Click on the background. Then select the **Sounds** tab. Select the **medieval2** sound from the library.

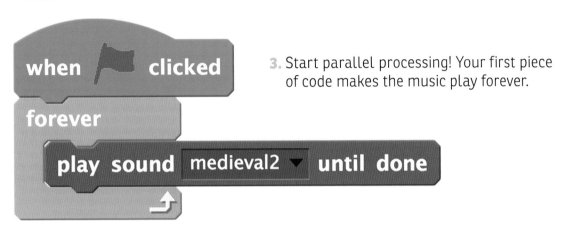

3. Start parallel processing! Your first piece of code makes the music play forever.

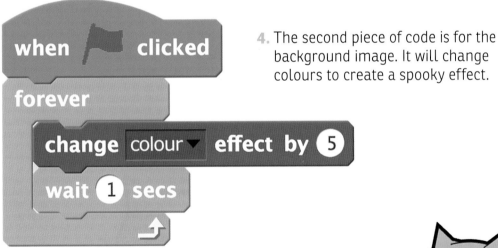

4. The second piece of code is for the background image. It will change colours to create a spooky effect.

TIP: If you want the colour to change more quickly, *decrease* the wait time in the forever loop. If you want the colour change to be more obvious, *increase* the number.

5. Now it is time to add the code onto the bat. This will make him move around the screen. Click on the **Bat2** sprite. Then select the **Scripts** tab and add this code:

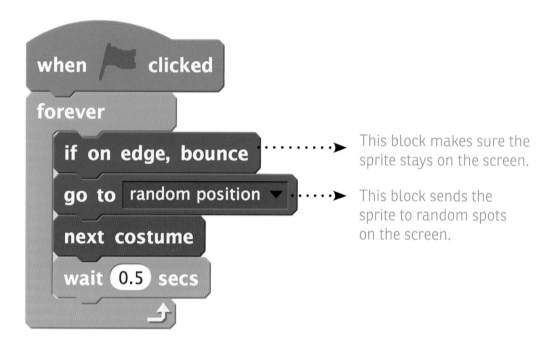

This block makes sure the sprite stays on the screen.

This block sends the sprite to random spots on the screen.

When you're ready, press the green flag. Your bat should disappear and re-appear around the screen. At the same time, the music will play and the background will flash.

TIP: Is the bat moving too quickly? *Increase* the wait time.

Add another sprite to the Spooky Scene.
Control it with the arrow keys.

TIP: Keep this page
handy! You'll need it
for future projects.

ARROW KEY CONTROLS

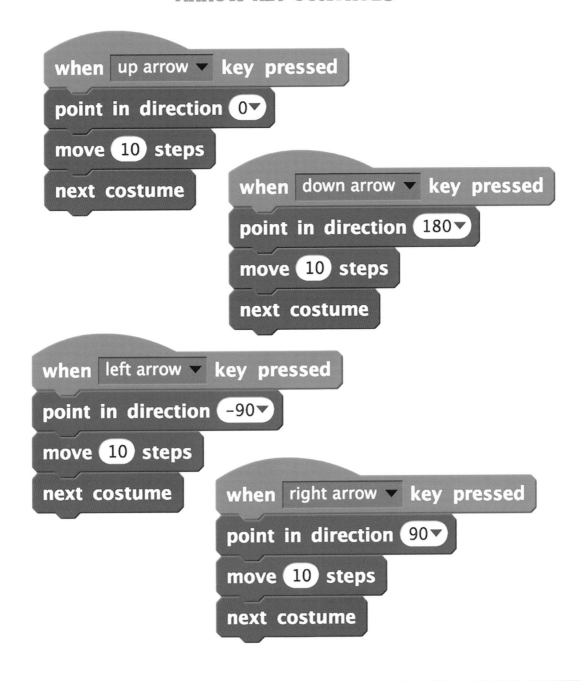

when [up arrow ▼] key pressed

point in direction (0 ▼)

move (10) steps

next costume

when [down arrow ▼] key pressed

point in direction (180 ▼)

move (10) steps

next costume

when [left arrow ▼] key pressed

point in direction (-90 ▼)

move (10) steps

next costume

when [right arrow ▼] key pressed

point in direction (90 ▼)

move (10) steps

next costume

SIMPLE SPINNER

Need a little variety? Try a random code block! These blocks are used when you want a program to run slightly differently each time.

One way to try out the random code blocks are by making a spinner. The spinners used for board games don't land on the same spot every time. Neither will yours! That's where the random code block comes in.

> pick random ① to ⑩

1. Select the **Arrow1** sprite from the sprite library.

Sprites

Arrow1

2. Use the paintbrush to create a multicoloured background. Divide it into quarters. Then fill in each square with a different colour.

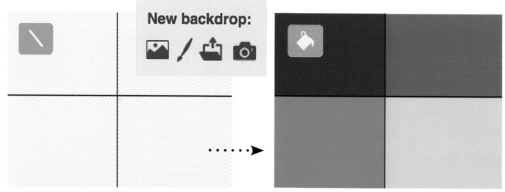

New backdrop:

TIP: Use black lines to separate the background into four sections. Then use the paint bucket to fill each square with a different colour.

3. Next, add code to the arrow sprite. This will make it spin.

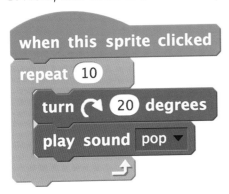

Select the **Arrow1** sprite. Place this code in the Scripts section.

This code is almost perfect! There's only one problem – the spinner will turn 10 times every time. You need your spinner to spin a random number of times. Fix it by adding the **random** block.

4. Go to the **Operators** category. Find the **pick random** block.

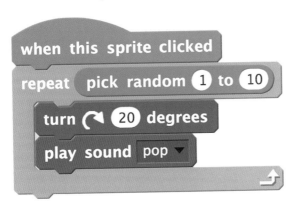

Drag the **pick random** block and drop onto the **repeat** block. Your program will now repeat a random number of times. It could repeat once, 10 times or any amount in between.

5. Change the numbers inside the **pick random** block. Start with 10 to 50.

6. Place the spinner in the middle of the colours. Then click it!

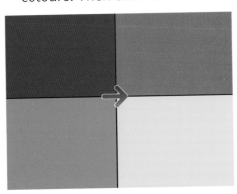

EXTRAS!

Play around with the random numbers that you've used for the spinner. Try adding a **random** block to the number of degrees the arrow turns. Another idea is to increase the number of degrees. **What happens to the speed of the arrow?**

OCEAN DODGE

If you take out a library book, you will need to return it. If you don't return it on time, you have to pay a fine. The results of each action are called conditions.

Coding also has conditions. You might want a certain event to take place, but only after another event has happened. If one thing happens, then you will program another action.

Try creating a condition with a win-or-lose scenario. You will code a shark that swims backwards and forwards. If the crab touches the shark, it starts all over again at the beginning. If it gets to the donut, the crab will win!

1. Select the **Crab**, **Donut** and **Shark** sprites. Choose the **Underwater3** background.

underwater3

2. Arrange the sprites on the background.

3. Click on the **Donut** sprite and add this code:

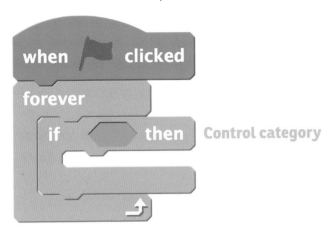

Control category

4. Select the **Sensing** category.
Find the **touching** block.

touching [mouse-pointer ▼] ?

5. Select **Crab** using the arrow.

touching [Crab ▼] ?

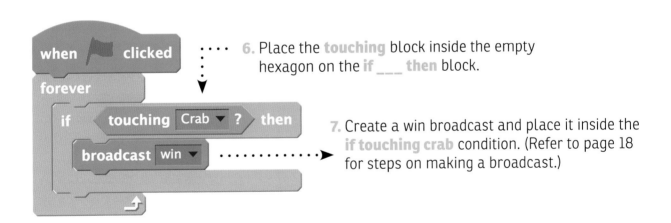

6. Place the **touching** block inside the empty hexagon on the **if ___ then** block.

7. Create a win broadcast and place it inside the **if touching crab** condition. (Refer to page 18 for steps on making a broadcast.)

TIP: The broadcast block is in the *Events* category.

8. Click on the **Shark** sprite. Add this code. It will make the shark move and react to the crab.

```
when [flag] clicked
forever
    move 10 steps
    if on edge, bounce
    if < touching [Crab ▼] ? > then
        broadcast [hit ▼]
```

The **move** and **bounce** tiles cause the shark to travel across the screen.

9. Click the **Crab** sprite. Add the arrow key control code found on page 15. Then find the **go to x: y:** block. This block changes the numbers next to x and y automatically, based on the location of your sprite. The x and y numbers create a **coordinate**. The coordinate is the sprite's exact location on the screen.

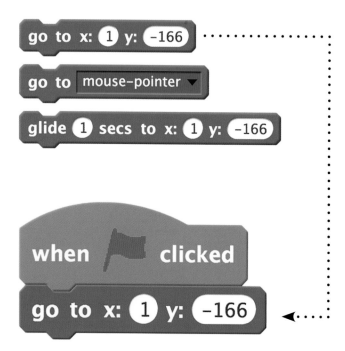

```
go to x: 1 y: -166

go to [mouse-pointer ▼]

glide 1 secs to x: 1 y: -166


when [flag] clicked
go to x: 1 y: -166
```

If the shark flips upside down, change the sprite's rotation style.

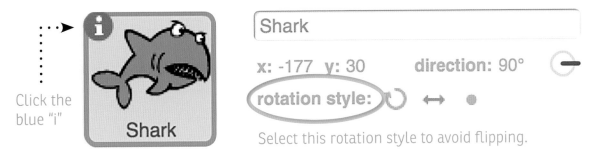

Click the blue "i"

Shark

Shark

x: -177 y: 30   direction: 90°

rotation style:

Select this rotation style to avoid flipping.

10. Code what happens when the crab receives both broadcasts. Then press the green flag and try your luck!

when I receive hit ▼
go to x: 1 y: -166
play sound kick drum ▼

This will send the crab back to his starting coordinate. Select the **kick drum** sound from the sound library.

when I receive win ▼
say Yummy Doughnut! for 2 secs
play sound dance celebrate ▼ until done

Select the **dance celebrate** sound from the sound library.

EXTRAS!

Add another moving sprite to dodge. Make the sprite move more quickly than the Shark. The code will be the same as the Shark's code. The only difference will be the move block. What do you think will happen if you change the number of steps the sprite takes?

CODE IS
A-MAZE-ING

There are so many things you can do with code! Have a sprite interact with or react to objects. For example, a sprite knows when it is touching a certain colour. You can code the sprite to run a program after it touches that colour. One example would be getting the sprite to change costumes after a muddy brown ball touches it. Yuck!

Let's code a beetle to move through a pink maze without touching it. If it touches the pink, it will be sent back to the beginning. If the beetle makes it to the Cheesy-Puffs, it wins!

1. Select the **Beetle** and **Cheesy-Puffs** sprites.

2. Add this code to the **Cheesy-Puffs** sprite:

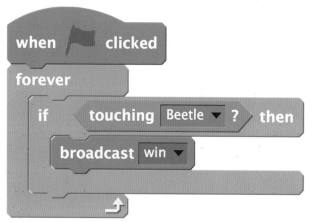

Need a reminder about how to put conditional code together? Visit page 37.

3. Create a maze background by using the drawing tools.

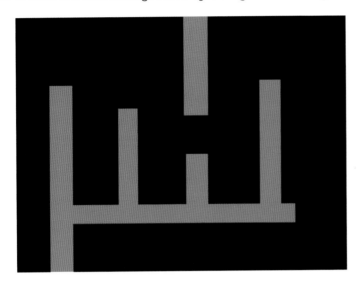

Use the rectangle tool to make the maze lines. Fill in the background with the paint bucket.

4. Place the **Beetle** and **Cheesy-Puffs** sprites on the background.

Use these tools to grow and shrink the sprites.

TIP: Stick to two colours when making the maze. This will help keep the colour detection code clear.

5. Add the arrow key control code on page 15 to the beetle. Then add this code:

```
when 🏳 clicked
go to x: -169 y: 134
point in direction 90▾
forever
    if ⟨ touching colour ▢ ? ⟩ then
        go to x: -169 y: 134
        play sound kick drum ▾ until done
```

Find the x and y numbers in the lower-right-hand side of the screen. Enter them in the two **go to x: y:** blocks.

```
⟨ touching colour ▢ ? ⟩
```

Find the touching colour block in **Sensing**. To select the colour of your maze, click the coloured square. A small hand will appear. Move it over to the colour you wish to select, then click.

6. Program what you want to happen when the **Beetle** reaches the **Cheesy-Puffs**.

```
when I receive win ▾
say I win!
play sound dance celebrate ▾ until done
```

7. Select the **dance celebrate** sound from the sound library. Then select it in the play sound block.

Add another sprite. Place it in the maze as an obstacle for the beetle to avoid. Touching the sprite will send the beetle back to the beginning.

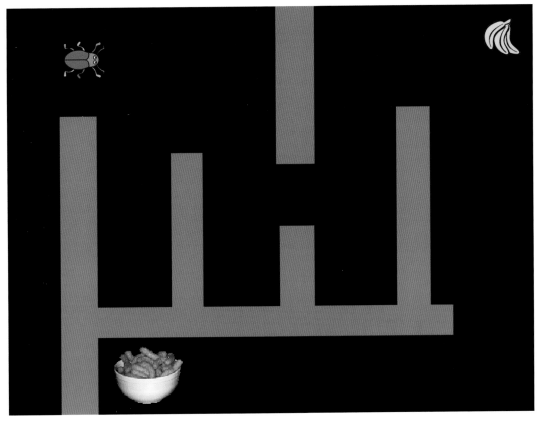

Bananas were added as an obstacle here!

TIP: The code for the obstacle will be an easy one. It's almost the same as the *if-then* conditional statement for when the beetle touches anything pink.

PIZZA PARTY

An elephant at a pizza party? That's crazy! You can count how much pizza it eats by setting a variable.

A variable is a space holder for a value. Its number can change. One example of a variable is your age. It changes every time you have a birthday. In this case, the variable goes up.

The elephant will move around the screen to collect all of the pizza. The variable you will be changing is the amount of pizza that the elephant has eaten.

1. Select the **Elephant** sprite. Use the drawing tools to create your own pizza sprite.

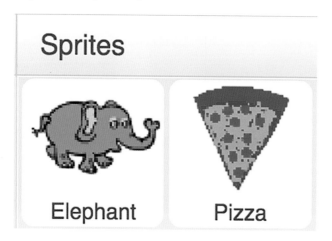

2. To name the sprite you created, click the "i" next to it. Then type the name in the white box.

Pizza

x: -155 y: 21   direction: 90°

rotation style: ↻ ↔ •

3. Select the **party room** background from the library.

1

party room
480x360

4. Make a second background using the drawing tools. This background will be shown when the elephant has eaten all the pizza.

I'm Full ◀· · · · · · · · · · · · · · · · · · · Name your background!

I'm Full!

T

Use the "T" tool to type on the background.

Use the paint bucket to colour the background.

5. Find the orange **Data** category of the code blocks. You will need to create a variable to keep track of the pizza eaten. Click the **make new variable** button. Then fill out the pop-up box.

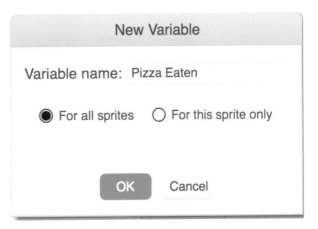

New Variable

Variable name: Pizza Eaten

● For all sprites   ○ For this sprite only

OK   Cancel

Check this box to see the variable on the project page. ·····▶ ☑  **Pizza Eaten**

6. You will now have access to new code blocks to use in your project.

set `Pizza Eaten ▼` to `0`

change `Pizza Eaten ▼` by `1`

show variable `Pizza Eaten ▼`

hide variable `Pizza Eaten ▼`

7. Add this code to the pizza sprite.

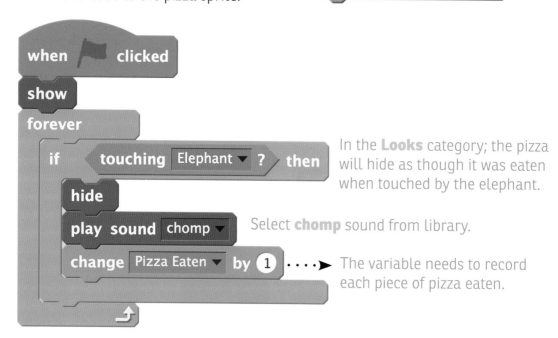

when 🏴 clicked

show

forever

  if ⟨ touching `Elephant ▼` ? ⟩ then

    hide

    play sound `chomp ▼`

    change `Pizza Eaten ▼` by `1` ····▶

In the **Looks** category; the pizza will hide as though it was eaten when touched by the elephant.

Select **chomp** sound from library.

The variable needs to record each piece of pizza eaten.

8. Use the stamp tool to copy the pizza sprite 4 times. Arrange the pieces on the screen.

When you copy a sprite that has code on it, the costume and code are copied too.

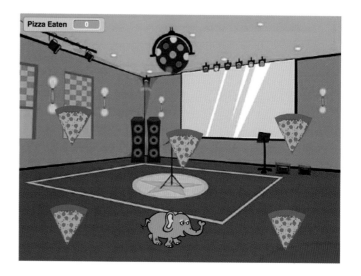

Pizza Eaten 0

9. Add the arrow key control code from page 15 to give the elephant movement. Then add the code below. Once the elephant has eaten all the pizza, the background will change to the **I'm Full** screen.

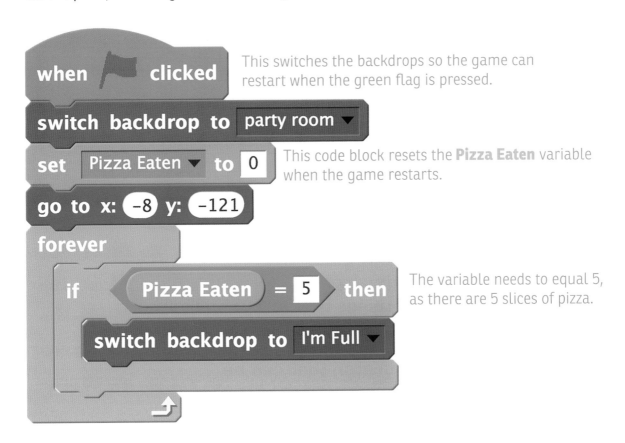

This switches the backdrops so the game can restart when the green flag is pressed.

This code block resets the **Pizza Eaten** variable when the game restarts.

The variable needs to equal 5, as there are 5 slices of pizza.

Place the **Pizza Eaten** variable inside this block to create the code above.

Find this block in the **Operators** category.

EXTRAS!

Add more food for the elephant to collect. You will need to make a new variable to track the new food. Create a third backdrop to switch to if the elephant eats all of the food!

GLOSSARY

code set of specific directions given to a computer in order for it to complete different tasks

conditional statement part of coding language that performs an action if another action takes place first

coordinate measurements used to identify an exact position

loop something repeated

sequence series of things that follow each other in a certain order

sprite anything in Scratch that can be programmed to move

variable something that can change

FIND OUT MORE

BOOKS

Coding for Beginners using Scratch: Simple Coding for Absolute Beginners, Jonathan Melmoth, Rosie Dickins and Louie Stowell (Usborne Books, 2016)

Computer Coding for Kids, Carol Vorderman (Dorling Kindersley, 2015)

How Coding Works (Our Digital Planet), Ben Hubbard (Raintree, 2017)

WEBSITES

www.bbc.co.uk/guides/zskthyc#zxg72hv
Create an animation using your own computer code.

www.dkfindout.com/uk/computer-coding/
Find out more about Scratch and other programming languages such as Python.

INDEX